VEGAN FAMILY

Written By Randi Seltzer Bonica

•

Illustrated By Abby Broussard

For Murray

For Adrian and Drake

 **V** is for the **vegetables**,
the fruit, the nuts, and the seeds.

STRAWBERRY

BLUEBERRIES

PEAS

CARROTS

BANANAS

We eat them for every meal and snack and get the nutrients we need.

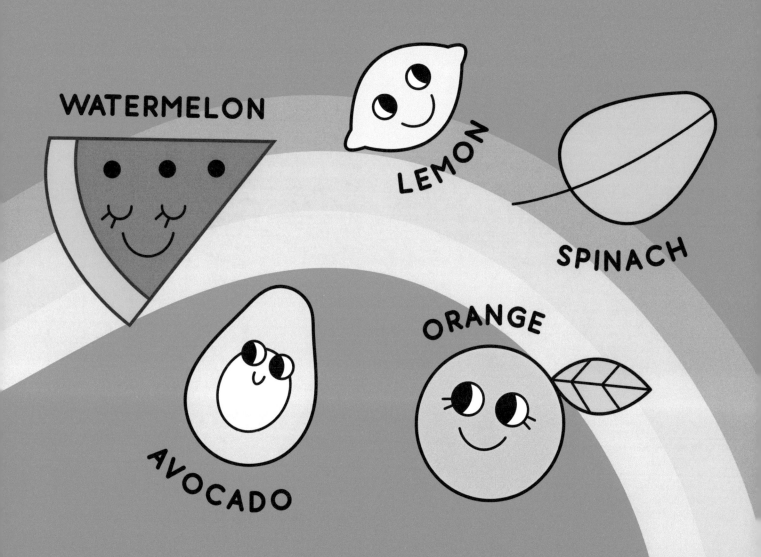

WATERMELON

LEMON

SPINACH

AVOCADO

ORANGE

 is for the **empathy**
we show for everything alive.

BIG

SMALL

Big and small, short and tall—
they all want to survive.

SHORT

TALL

G  is for feeling **grateful** for the vegan foods we eat.

CHERRY

BREAD

GRAPES

YUM

CORN

CAKE

BROCCOLI

Animals have feelings just like us and aren't dairy, eggs, or meat.

 is for the **animals**.
We are vegan just for them.

We don't believe our taste buds
are more important than our friends.

N is for saying, "**No thanks,**" which can be really rough.

Not everyone sees the world our way, and sometimes it feels tough.

F is for the **freedom** we hope they see one day.

LET US

No animals will be jailed or hurt;
they can all live and play.

A is for feeling **alone**,
which all vegans sometimes do.
It's hard to be a little different
at a party or at school.

It's going to be okay.

I is for the **ice cream**.
Of course we eat that too.

ALMOND

It comes from nuts, plants, and seeds
and not our friends who moo.

L is for the **love** in our vegan family.

We think about being kind
and letting the animals be free.

Y is for **you**, my love,
because you will have a choice.

You'll grow up proud, strong, and brave, and the world will hear your voice.

About the Author

Randi Seltzer Bonica is a vegan mama, a high school guidance counselor, an animal advocate, and a jewelry maker. She lives with her husband Steve, her son, Murray, and her six rescue cats in Rockaway Beach, New York City.

About the Illustrator

Abby Broussard is the owner and artist behind a small vegan business specializing in flair and apparel. When she's not illustrating silly pictures, she enjoys spending time with her husband, Ross, and her two sons, Adrian and Drake. Abby resides in Austin, Texas.

Archway Publishing books may be ordered through booksellers or by contacting:

Archway Publishing
1663 Liberty Drive
Bloomington, IN 47403
www.archwaypublishing.com
844-669-3957

Because of the dynamic nature of the Internet, any web addresses or links contained in this book may have changed since publication and may no longer be valid. The views expressed in this work are solely those of the author and do not necessarily reflect the views of the publisher, and the publisher hereby disclaims any responsibility for them.

ISBN: 978-1-6657-0010-8 (sc)
ISBN: 978-1-6657-0011-5 (hc)
ISBN: 978-1-6657-0009-2 (e)

Print information available on the last page.

Archway Publishing rev. date: 04/08/2021

ARCHWAY
PUBLISHING

Printed in the United States
by Baker & Taylor Publisher Services